www.finishinglinepress.com

Let You Fly

New Women's Voices Series, No. 138

poems by

Susan Okie

Finishing Line Press
Georgetown, Kentucky

Let You Fly

New Women's Voices Series, No. 138

ACKNOWLEDGMENTS

I would like to thank the following publications and venues, where these
poems first appeared, sometimes in different form:

Beltway Poetry Quarterly: "After the Mammogram."
Cider Press Review: "Elizabeth Bishop Injects Herself with Adrenaline for
Asthma."
Gargoyle: "Thy Bed of Crimson Joy."
Innisfree Poetry Journal: "Let You Fly."
The Journal of the American Medical Association: "Ignacio's Foot."

"Perseid" won first prize in the 2012 Bethesda Poetry Contest (judged by
poet Michael Collier) and was published on the blog of The Writer's Center,
located in Bethesda, Maryland.
"Slippery" was selected by poet Merrill Leffler for outdoor display on a metal
poster as part of the 2016 Takoma Park Poetry Walk, sponsored by Friends
of the Takoma Park, Maryland, Library.

My thanks to my teachers, Joan Aleshire, Marianne Boruch, Maurice
Manning, Stanley Plumly, and Alan Shapiro; to my poetry community,
especially the La Madeleine poets; and to my husband, Walter Weiss, who
reads my work with an artist's eye.

Publisher: Leah Maines
Editor: Christen Kincaid
Cover Art: Terry Donsen Feder
Author Photo: Gavin Courtney
Cover Design: Shanna Compton

Printed in the USA on acid-free paper.
Order online: www.finishinglinepress.com
also available on amazon.com

Author inquiries and mail orders:
Finishing Line Press
P. O. Box 1626
Georgetown, Kentucky 40324
U. S. A.

Table of Contents

For Walter, Peter and Jacob

Elizabeth Bishop Injects Herself with Adrenaline for Asthma

A fine needle in the arm opens your chest,
raises you to a high pitch,
sets you humming all night.
Saved from drowning, you float
on the surface, gulping breaths,
heart at a Scarlatti gallop—
and how the lines come in a fine
tremble as your fingers grip the pen
to make illegible stitches
on the moon-white.

Lend me your waterfall. I want
to watch the fireflies floating
up the wooded ridge at Samambaia,
to hear your gardener, Manuelinho,
singing to his donkey. Let me dive
with the riverman, to the place
where Luandinha, the serpent goddess,
will blow her cigar smoke into my mouth.

Transformer

I was a propeller,
whirling on short legs,
hands grasping one end of a rake,
clipped grass blurring by, weight
pulling my arms, spinning me
faster as I watched teeth fly
past walnut tree, fence, house, garage.

The back door slammed.
I saw him coming, tilting
in his baby walk and calling.
I knew if he got too close I'd rake him,
didn't want to stop. He kept coming
and I didn't slow until I felt the rake skip
across his forehead and he screamed.
Dizzy, the red blur of his blood
shining, spreading.

How those teeth's delicious pull
made me huge, sharp,
spun my giant,
drew him in
until I couldn't take it back.

The Ears

Ears are telltale, said Grandmother,
pouring stories into mine:

One night, at boarding school in Florida,
a girl opened a jewelry box to show me
a black man's ear
wrapped in cotton wool,
hoarded like a rabbit's foot.
I stared but didn't dare ask
how she'd come by it,
why she kept it.

And once, she talked to me about the Jews—
they owned such a lot,
even ran the movie business:

Something should be done.
Look at their ears,
you draw a line from lobe to nose
and if the lobe is lower,
then you know.

Know what?
We rode into the Alps to see
where Hitler and his officers had lived—
a bad man, she said, he caused the war,
but wouldn't say how.

That night, puppets sang about love,
secrets and a magic flute,
the Queen of the Night trilled her fury—

my only daughter, lost,
and with her, all my luck…
an evil man stole her from me—

her notes hot needles
searing my ears.

Let You Fly

Panis angelicus, we sang,
Sister in her wimple and veil
sweeping her arms in arcs,
shaping the Latin with full lips.

The soul a circle she drew
on the blackboard, grace the side
of the chalk shading it white,
sin the eraser, rubbing
grace out, turning the soul black.
You had to make a perfect act
of contrition in case you died
in your sleep.

My mother heard me crying,
sat on my bed in her nylon nightgown,
held me: *I'm not going to die
for a long time.* Other families
were the ones with problems.
When she cried, she always
locked the bathroom door.

Old photos show her in a spotlight,
singing with a big band before the war.
*When your time comes to leave the nest,
I hope I'll let you fly.*

Bread of angels, melting in my mouth,
tasting of her voice.

Auction Pony

She's not one of those who splay their feet
and sink to the ground, trying to get away.
She stands strong, slender legs under her,
head erect on a long neck, looking
at the crowd with a questioning eye.
Palomino with ragged spots of cream,
shining in cloud-filtered light,
owning her body. Forward in small, smooth steps
into the arena, as if two strong men
were not gripping her by the chest and haunches.

Pretty as they come,
booms the amplified voice of the auctioneer.
Who'll start the bidding at one thousand?

Into the center they urge her,
pivot her to face the faces
while another looks for bidders, shouts
at a raised hand. The price climbs fast:
she's tall, golden, all can sense
her spirit. She can't know that beauty, heart,
even that pale coat, have marked her
to become a brood mare on the refuge.
Tomorrow, when other foals are loaded into trailers
to learn about the bit for some child's pleasure,
she'll wade into the channel with the wild herd,
swim back to the island with her mother.

Undertaking

The front parlor was wide and still,
reserved for wakes, forbidden
to the children, who weren't to know.

Go play at your aunt's, he'd order them,
before bringing a body in.

A big, red-faced man, cellar voice,
hug scratchy and too tight,
stubborn jaw, shiny glasses hiding

his eyes, laugh a roar—
my mother's father, who undertook
to take you under.

Once, as a girl, my mother hid at the top
of the stairs—*what's in that big black box?*
why can't I see?—

and crept down to peek:
a nun, white skin, black veil
and habit, neither female nor male.

In her dream, the nun sat up
and chased her as a man.
What did her father tell her then, I wonder?

A beautiful voice, all she ever said
about her mother, Margaret, who lay upstairs
the year she started music school,

sick with Hodgkin's. Weekends, Mother
caught rides home, past snowy farms,
to watch her die.

My Parents Picnic on Corregidor

Noon light from beyond the rough pavilion
almost blinds the camera. Thicketed
by jungle grasses taller than a man,
five officers, fading to whites and grays,
are eating in a mess hall where their enemies
once took their meals. I see paper fringe
still hanging from a beam—temple banner,
prayer flag? A WAC in a striped shirt,
her blond hair blurred in the foreground.
The sunlit ear of a major, back
to the lens. That square-jawed guy
is Mitchell, the camera's owner, sipping
from a mug. But I can't stop staring
at a man looking down through wire rims,
hair much fuller than I ever knew it.
Father—young, bare-chested in the heat,
with that familiar air of being elsewhere.
A day's leave, the war a month over.

There she is, mother, dark curl straggling
down her forehead, turned away from him.
Her eyes accuse the camera, sandwich up
to hide her mouth, while he, ropy-muscled,
grabs an olive. They're shaded by shingles
laid across the shelter's ruined roof.
What do they talk about, away from tents
and typewriters, their long work of transcribing
captured soldiers almost done?
Australian beers and canned turkey—
the chow absorbed us pretty thoroughly,
my father scrawled. Snapshots, mailed home.
First date, maybe. She black Irish, skinny
—all those Lucky Strikes—and I know
she's trying not to show her crooked teeth.

Would anyone, not knowing what came later,
spot a hint of chemistry between them?
They never spoke of how they fell in love,
or the war. He did recall, once, thinking,
over beers beneath a tree, *a pretty neat kid.*
That's all I got from him, no matter how I asked.
Another shot: she's laughing, but bending
forward, hugging her chest—so lovely,
yet can't forget the camera, as if her body
might betray her. Someone in New York
broke her heart before the war, she said
(trying to warn me off sex). Did she see him
as safe, quiet, self-contained, yet teasing
with the sudden flash of wit?
My father's eyes, only for his sandwich.
I wish he'd turn and smile at her.

Final pose: father and the women
in their Army shirts, windblown, on a boat,
sea and sky whited out. Too faint
for me to overhear, and years too late
to ask for the story. Now, mother leans
against him with a smile, and he
looks at the camera, grinning. Young, arrested,
unknowable as gods on a temple wall.

Those summer evenings after supper,

the striped sofa with its curving back
and stiff-soft arms was the lap
where my father hid his face.
When I was small, he'd measure
bourbon in a shiny steel jigger.
Later, straight into the glass, sip, add more,
never draining the bottle—no,
withdrawing just enough to get gone.

The sound track was Vin Scully,
voice of the Los Angeles Dodgers,
calling the game on the Magnavox.
Mom had it on in the kitchen, too,
but clattered supper dishes loud enough
to drown out half the plays.
My brother listened, stretched out on his bed,
maybe planning to sneak out later
to smoke a joint. Nowhere in the house
could I escape that genial voice
covering our silence.

In the Anatomy Lab

I was behind in my dissecting—
I'd spent too long tracing nerves
in the embalmed gray skin of her forearm.
That night, I unwrapped
only her right hand and sat, probing
to free the lovely network of cables
in her palm. I didn't know her name,
 or one thing about her life.

When I tugged on the *flexor digitorum* tendons,
her fingers partly closed and her thumb
crooked in. I seemed to see the two of us
as if from outside, and could no longer
name the tendons. I felt my fingers
from inside her hand.

Soon I would open the gates of her ribs,
would hold even her heart in my palm.
Afterward, always, home, to feel yours
circling on the small of my back.

Learning to Drink

Bourbon was my father's.
So I tried Scotch and felt cool
when it burned my tongue
and washed over my brain
like a slow incoming tide.

White wine was training wheels—
cheap, fruity, easy to ride.
I drank it with my first boyfriend
when sex was still strange
and I needed help falling into it.

Martinis were too strong,
my mother warned. I'd order one
with a friend in a Beacon Street bar
for the shape of its glass, the spin,
a feeling of flawlessness.

High-grade Haitian rum cured
the ache of a day at the microscope
looking for malaria on blood slides
in a hospital that smelled of women
who'd walked miles carrying a child.

Scotch after every ER shift, to slow
my racing mind—not over what I'd seen
but from fear of what I might see next.
Woman hemorrhaging into her stomach.
Church lady whose asthma stops her breath.

And Scotch after picking up the baby
at the sitter's, plunking him in his high chair,
spooning out strained carrots, warming
his bottle, reaching for my own. Craving it
like the smell of his fine hair.

Thy Bed of Crimson Joy

Yellow skin, belly taut
and round—a lemon
of a man. *Doctor,* he'd call,
I need a beer. We found a few,
one time, under his bed. His mother
sneaked them in, although she knew
beer had done in his liver, beer
would kill him. *Doctor…* One day,
I heard a different note, found him
struggling to sit up while dark blood
gushed from his throat.
He reached for me, eyes wide
as a child's. I shouted, ran for help,
but all refused to come:
Nothing to save.
I found his breathing stilled,
a lemon on a crimson bed.

The Rainy Season Begins in Western Kenya

She leaps over stones, laughing,
her teeth white in the dusk,
as if crossing a stream by stepping
only in water.

All the stones have gaping mouths
and sticky tongues waiting
for the long-winged termites
rising out of their mounds,
drawn from earth into sky
by the coming of the long rains

to swarm over rutted roads,
gardens and slums,
rice fields and marshes
and, as they seek to mate, to fly
into the beaks of sacred ibises
and lilac-breasted rollers,
into the mouths of dust-colored mutts
and stone-colored toads,

even into Judith's,
who doesn't stop laughing as she jumps
over the last toad and enters
the kitchen, her dress soaked through.

Slippery

The hinge, crusted with mud,
resists your effort,
so you twist and saw,
cut through the crack,
turning a line into
a mouth helplessly opening.
You pry the shells apart
to show gray flesh
glistening in its sea water
and you pass it to me.
I tip the bed and slide
the cold body onto my tongue—
like the afterbirth
of a mermaid: salty,
so mellifluous that I
swallow it whole.

Autumn

Rising out of earth, stars
caught in wet meadows.

Smell of loam released,
autumn in the throat—

Orion with his belt and bow hunts
where the does are feeding.

After the Mammogram

Now that a pale algal smudge has been caught
in the net, faint against the black,
a letter arrives—*more images needed.*
The words wake me as if I were a carp
dreaming of being hauled out
of the shadows under the lilies.
Chill, I tell the fish, it's only
a call-back, probably nothing.
But someone has cast a stone over me,
ripples move across the surface,
erasing a view of the sky.

A Dead Loon

Delicate black feet, webbed twigs,
the sharp beak black above, white below,
the body sea-smoothed, feathers speckled
in fine white circles on a black ground.
No wound. Not a quill disturbed.
It lies where the tide laid it
on the dry marsh grass, sculptural, inexplicable,
soft as patterned snow, no doubt teeming
with feather lice and microbes feasting,
but nothing yet to mar the outer form.

It's duck season, the salt-soup end of the year.
Birds chuckle across the water, tucked up
in the brown marsh, everything looking far
and sounding near. From somewhere beyond
the woods I hear the honking of the flock
of snow geese, invisible but in my mind
a blinding white, a multitude—and I seem
to make out single voices, all saying the same thing.

Ignacio's Foot

I know this foot, the sturdy stump
that ends mid-instep in a callused knob,
the horny yellow skin slammed with each step
against the sole of your salted working boot.
I remember toes turning dusky
like summer plums, the innocent-looking wound
launching bacteria to melt your flesh.
On your X-rays, infection's shadow
crept up the bones till I sent you
by taxi to the hospital, where a surgeon
lopped off the darkened, rotting half.

Mornings, since your daughter took you in,
you limp beside your grandson to the bus,
clean the house, scrape together dollars
to pay your fare. Today, you greet me
with a toothless smile and show your numbers—
high-water marks of sugar in the blood.
Tenderly, you unswaddle the stump,
present it for my inspection:
Look, perfecto! Next time
you see me here, I will walk in
with a woman on my arm.

Self-Portrait, 7:30 a.m.

Not for spite, but to mark the line
between you and me that I'm forever
tracing and rubbing out
like a dog who lies down
only to jump back up,
I stayed on the porch while you
went out to feel the sun
on your belly and legs
and, when they were warm,
to jump into the cold channel.

I won't go with you, not
while I'm still waiting for coffee
and can't think or speak.
When I go, it will be to sit listening
to water rippling against the pilings
and fish crows calling.

Pneumonia

Down at the building site, a wheel
grinds earth and rock, pouring
a stream of dust that coats the slope.

In father's last years, chained
to breath, he leaned forward,
lips pursed, in his green armchair.
In—out—in—out, hour on hour till bed.
Nights worse, spells of drowning.
My mother would call the EMTs.
Lucky Strikes, three packs a day—
his own fault, I thought then.
Now, I'm thinking of the war in the Pacific,
how those cigarettes got him through.

In my throat, a wheel rattles, catches
when I try to go deep. Where air
should be, a stone.

Perseid

The galaxy's rim spins
above, silver churning
on starless black.
Three of us in plastic chairs,
wearing all we brought, legs
under a quilt, tipping back.
That dark
is interstellar dust,
says my husband, not *nothing*.
I choose a black hole
in the wild white river,
and let my eyes unfocus
till stars at my vision's edge
brighten and burn.
A rushing spark,
its wake glowing, vanishing.
Under the blanket, Jacob
squeezes my hand. Nothing—
no, another spark, another,
and on our right a flash
aims right for us
and goes out, burned to ash.

At Mount Rainier

An Octopus
of ice, Marianne Moore called
the tentacles that crept down
the mountain's flanks: now hacked away
or dwindling at the head of a moraine.
On this south side, the dome
gleams white with sunspots,
black wens of rock bared by melting.
Nisqually's ice slumps on a shoulder,
soiled cat trailing a muddy scarf.
Where snow once stayed, a stream
cuts through a lunar plain of stones,
the banks all moss and monkeyflowers.
More than fifty years ago, my father
drove us all day around—
on every side, rivers of ice.

Twenty-six, the official glacier census.
When Moore hiked here
in 1922, the count was twenty-eight,
yet a pink-faced ranger insists
none has been lost. In a century,
he admits, *they'll all go,*
we're losing ten centimeters a day
of Nisqually, hoping the metric system
will muffle this news.

                    Up on the trail,
a father lures a jay to snatch crackers
from a child's hand for a video.
Another leads teenage sons past
a barrier to tramp across a meadow.
A wife and husband take turns pushing
their grown daughter's wheelchair
up the paved path to Myrtle Falls. Above
our heads, a whine like a power saw,
and we spot a drone against the blue.
Go! cries a small girl as her father
nudges her to let us pass.

Hide and Seek

Fog smudging pines across the water,
shifting how I read things.

At the dock's end I enter cloud until,
to a watcher, my shape must blur

like our last visit, father. You, recovering
from fever, ashamed I'd flown

all that way. For once, you felt
like talking. *Ask me anything.*

Me, stone-tongue, five months gone,
the baby shifting in my belly.

Notes

The title "Thy Bed of Crimson Joy" is taken from "The Sick Rose" by William Blake.

In "The Ears," lines 27-29 are from the Queen of the Night's aria in Act 1, Scene 6 of *The Magic Flute* by Wolfgang Amadeus Mozart. The translation is mine.

Susan Okie is a poet, a doctor, and a former *Washington Post* medical reporter and science editor. Her work has appeared in *The Gettysburg Review, Prairie Schooner, The Bellevue Literary Review, the Journal of the American Medical Association, The Cider Press Review, Gargoyle, Beltway Poetry Quarterly, Innisfree Poetry Journal, Passager,* and *Hospital Drive.* She is a graduate of the Warren Wilson MFA Program for Writers.

Susan grew up in Los Angeles and settled on the east coast after college and medical school. She spent almost two decades on the staff of the *Post,* reporting as a freelancer from Africa during three years when her family lived in western Kenya. She later served as a contributing editor for the *New England Journal of Medicine.*

A clinical assistant professor of family medicine at Georgetown University Medical School, she teaches patient interviewing and clinical ethics to first-year and second-year medical students, and volunteers at a clinic for uninsured adults in Montgomery County, Md.

She is the author of two nonfiction books, *Fed Up,* a book about childhood obesity, and *To Space and Back,* a children's book coauthored with the late astronaut Sally Ride. She lives with her husband in Bethesda, Md.

You can find out more about her poetry at susanokie.com.

CPSIA information can be obtained
at www.ICGtesting.com
Printed in the USA
LVOW12s0358170218
566818LV00002BB/2/P